SIMPLY SCIENCE

Sound

by Darlene R. Stille

Content Advisers: Terrence E. Young Jr., M.Ed., M.L.S., Jefferson Parish (La.) Public Schools, and Janann Jenner, Ph.D.

Reading Adviser: Dr. Linda D. Labbo, Department of Reading Education, College of Education, The University of Georgia

COMPASS POINT BOOKS

Minneapolis, Minnesota

Compass Point Books
151 Good Counsel Drive, P.O. Box 669
Mankato, MN 56002-0669

Visit Compass Point Books on the Internet at *www.compasspointbooks.com* or e-mail your request to *custserv@compasspointbooks.com*

Photographs ©:
Arthur Tilley/FPG International, cover; Jeff Greenberg/Visuals Unlimited, 4; Cheryl A. Ertelt, 5; Photo Network/Mark Newman, 6; Photo Network/Chad Ehlers, 7; T. Kitchin/Tom Stack and Associates, 8; Photo Network/Myrleen Ferguson Cate, 9 (top); Jeff Greenberg/Visuals Unlimited, 9 (bottom), 15; Unicorn Stock Photo/Aneal Vohra, 10 (top), 26; Pictor, 10 (bottom); Tom Stack/Tom Stack and Associates, 11; Novastock/Tom Stack and Associates, 12; Jim Cummins/FPG International, 16; David Falconer, 17, 25; A.J. Copley/Visuals Unlimited, 18; Unicorn Stock Photo/Tom McCarthy, 19, 23, 27; William L. Wantland/Tom Stack and Associates, 20; Photo Network/Tom Campbell, 22; Marilyn Moseley LaMantia, 24; Photo Network/Henryc T. Kaiser, 28 (left); Photo Network/Michael W. Thomas, 28 (right); Pictor/John Zoiner, 29.

Editors: E. Russell Primm, Emily J. Dolbear, and Melissa Stewart
Photo Researcher: Svetlana Zhurkina
Photo Selector: Matthew Eisentrager-Warner
Designer: Bradfordesign, Inc.

Library of Congress Cataloging-in-Publication Data

Stille, Darlene R.
Sound / by Darlene Stille.
p. cm. — (Simply science)
Includes bibliographical references and index.
ISBN-13: 978-0-7565-0092-4 (hardcover : lib. bdg.)
ISBN-10: 0-7565-0092-3 (hardcover : lib. bdg.)
ISBN-13: 978-0-7565-0978-1 (paperback)
ISBN-10: 0-7565-0978-5 (paperback)
1. Sound—Juvenile literature. [1. Sound.] I. Title. II. Simply science (Minneapolis, Minn.)
QC225.5 .S75 2001
534—dc21 00-010943

Printed in the United States of America.

Table of Contents

Listen!

Stop and listen. What do you hear? Do you hear people talking? Do you hear cars outside? Maybe you hear a bird chirping or a radio. Everything you hear is a sound.

Listening to an outdoor concert

Birds make beautiful sounds.

We hear many kinds of sounds. Some sounds are beautiful. Music is a beautiful sound. Some sounds are just noise. Cars and trucks make noisy sounds.

Traffic means loud sounds.

Orchestras play both loud and soft music.

Some sounds are loud. An airplane makes a loud noise. A band can play loud music. Some sounds are soft. A whisper is a soft sound. The wind blowing through the trees can make a soft sound.

You can measure how loud a sound is. Loudness is measured in **decibels**. A whisper may be only a few decibels. Talking to a friend may be about 60 decibels. A rock concert can be 115 to 120 decibels. A jet airplane taking off can be as loud as 140 decibels.

Airplanes create high decibels.

Making Sounds

All sounds come from **vibrations**. When something moves back and forth quickly, it vibrates. You can see some things vibrate. A guitar string moves back and forth when someone plucks it. Look closely and you can see the string vibrate. You can feel some things vibrate. The top of a drum moves back and forth when someone hits it.

Guitar strings vibrate when plucked.

Drummers

Put your hand on top of the drum and you can feel it vibrate. The **vocal cords** in your throat move back and forth when you speak or sing. Cars make noise when parts in the engine vibrate.

Singing moves your vocal cords.

Everything that moves causes vibrations. Everything that moves makes a sound.

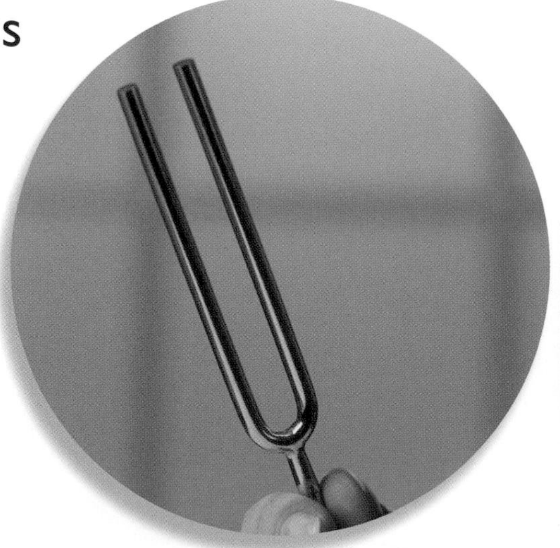

A vibrating tuning fork helps in tuning a piano.

Waves of Sound

Vibrations make waves of sound. Sound waves can move through air or water or metal. Sound can move through anything that vibrates. Most of the sound waves you hear move through the air. Then they move through your ear.

The air is often filled with sound waves.

You cannot see sound waves. But you can picture what sound waves look like. Sound waves look a bit like waves in water. What happens if you throw a stone into a lake or pond? Waves go out in circles from where the stone hit the water. Sound waves-go out in circles too. They go out from a drum or a violin or a car. They go out from whatever is vibrating.

Sound waves move out in circles much like waves of water.

Speed of Vibrations

Things that vibrate fast make many sound waves. These sound waves are close together. Things that vibrate slowly make fewer waves. These waves are farther apart.

You can count how many times something vibrates every second. This is called the **frequency** of the sound waves.

When many sound waves vibrate close together, they have a high frequency. Fewer sound waves vibrating farther apart have a low frequency.

This machine shows sound frequency on a screen.

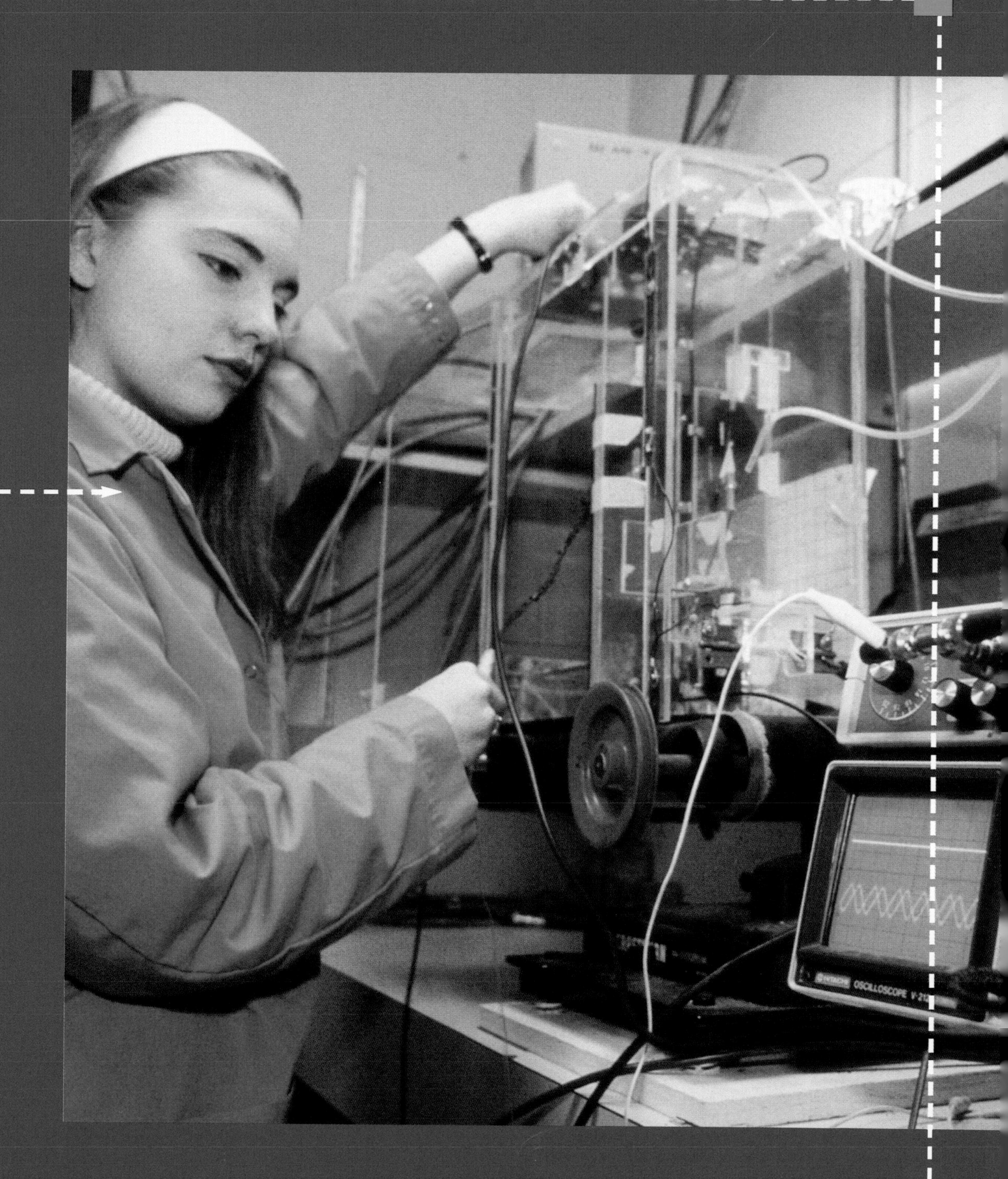
OSCILLOSCOPE

Some sounds are high and some sounds are low. This is called **pitch**. A violin or a flute can make high-pitched sounds. A bass or a trombone makes low-pitched sounds.

Flutes make high-pitched sounds.

A trombone player makes low-pitched sounds.

High-pitched sounds come from high-frequency sound waves. A violin string that vibrates very fast gives off many vibrations every second. This makes a high-pitched sound.

Low-pitched sounds come from low-frequency sound waves. A string on a bass that vibrates slowly makes a low-pitched sound.

Larger instruments usually make much lower sounds.

Sound Travels

Sound waves can travel. Soft sounds travel only a short way. The sounds you make when you talk do not go far. A person across the street could not hear you talking to a friend. Loud sounds travel a long way.

Sound waves move through the air faster than most airplanes. But light moves even faster. Nothing travels faster than light.

Sound doesn't travel far when you talk softly.

During a thunderstorm, you usually see lightning before you hear thunder. Thunder is the sound that lightning makes. You see the flashing light before the loud boom because light travels faster than sound.

If you hear thunder and see lightning at almost the same time, the storm is very close. If you hear thunder several seconds after you see lightning, the storm is many miles away.

Lightning during a thunderstorm

Hearing Sound

Why can you hear sound? You can hear sound because you have ears. Parts of your ears are outside your head. Parts of your ears are inside your head.

Sounds travel to your ear.

Radio music goes from your outer ear to your eardrum.

What happens when you listen to radio music? Sound waves from the radio hit the outside part of your ear. The sound goes into your head through a small opening in your outer ear. Your inside ear has a part called an **eardrum**.

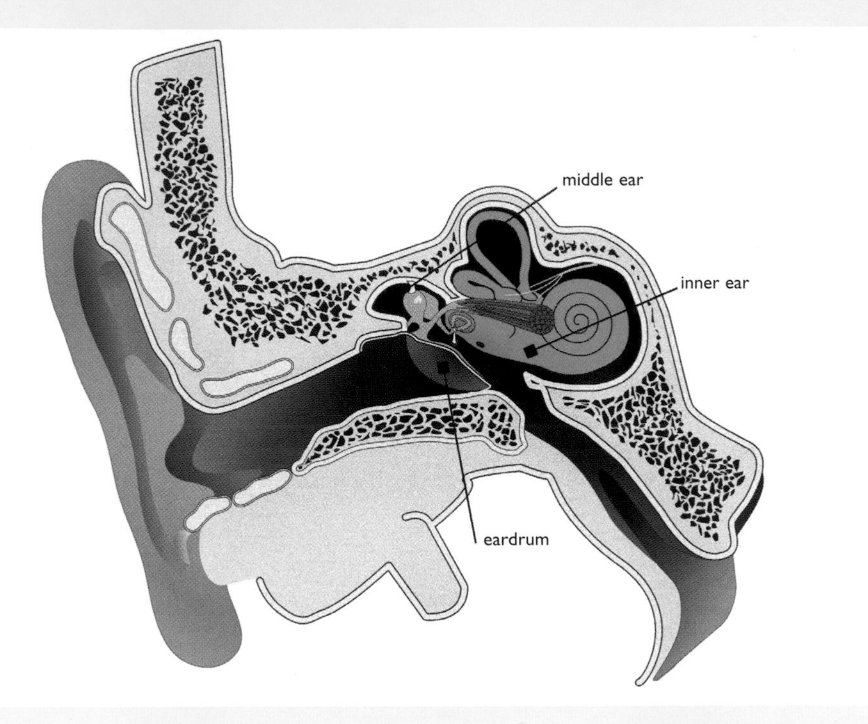

A diagram of the outer and inner ear

When sound waves hit your eardrum, it starts to vibrate. The vibrations move deeper inside your ear. They travel through your middle ear into your inner ear. **Nerves** in your inner ear carry a message to your brain. Your brain tells you, "That is my favorite song."

Using Sound

You use sound all the time. Sound lets you hear your friends when they talk to you. Sound lets you listen to music and hear people talking on television.

Sounds let you enjoy music.

Some sounds can save your life. A fire alarm can warn you to get out of a burning building. A honking car horn can tell you to stay on the curb.

Fire alarms help in emergencies.

Doctors use ultrasound to monitor pregnant women.

Special kinds of sound waves can even let you see things. For this you need a very-high-frequency sound called ultrasound. You cannot hear ultrasound.

Ultrasound waves help doctors see the shape of parts inside your body. A special machine is used for ultrasound. The pictures are shown on a television screen.

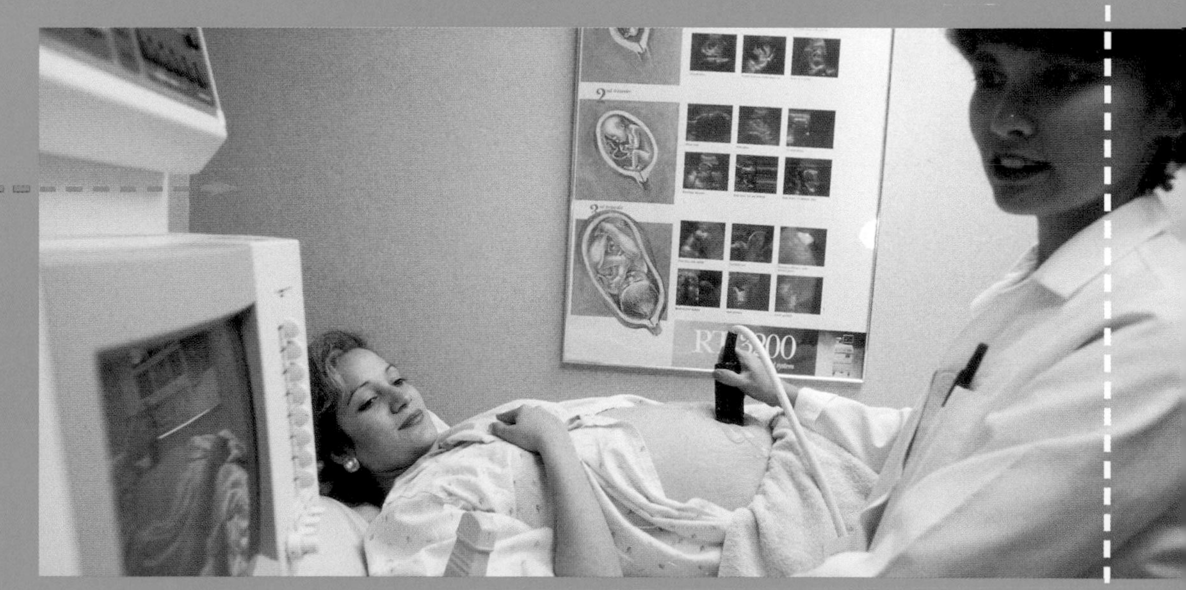

Take Care of Your Ears

It is very important to take care of your ears and your hearing. If your ears hurt, tell an adult. Medicine can make your ears feel better.

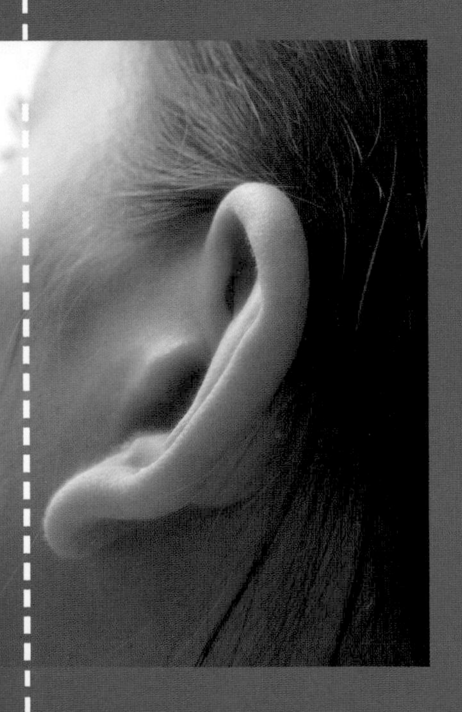

Hearing makes our lives richer.

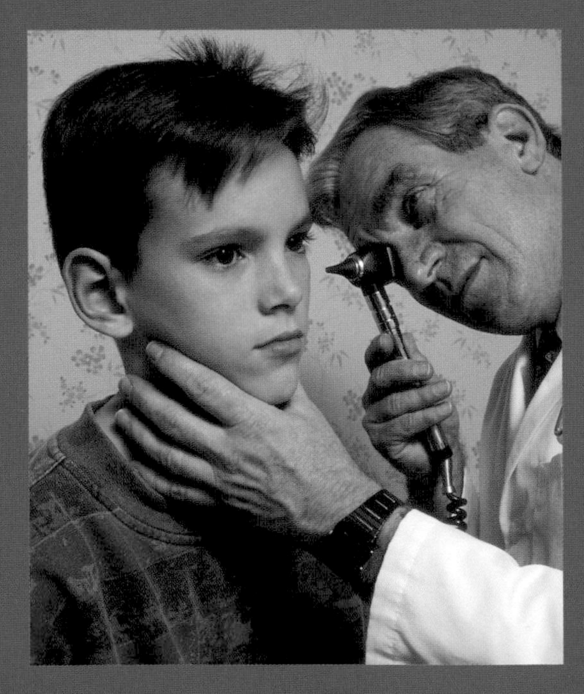

Ear exams help us stay healthy.

Loud noises can hurt your ears. They damage the tiny hairs in your ears that carry sound messages to your brain. That's why you shouldn't play music too loud. Many people who work around loud machines wear earplugs to protect their ears.

Always take care of your ears. They are very important. Your ears let you hear the world around you.

A factory worker wearing earplugs

Glossary

decibels—units that measure the loudness of sound

eardrum—a thin layer of skin inside your ear that vibrates

frequency—a measure of vibrations over a period of time

nerves—body parts that carry messages to and from the brain

pitch—a measure of sound that depends on its frequency. High-frequency sound waves create a high-pitched sound.

vibrations—back-and-forth movement

vocal cords—structures in your throat. They vibrate when you make sounds, such as talking and singing.

Did You Know?

- In 1947, a pilot named Chuck Yeager became the first person to travel faster than sound.
- The ears of a lizard, a robin, and a human being all work the same way.
- Sound can travel easily through solid ground.

Want to Know More?

At the Library

Madgwick, Wendy. *Super Sound.* Austin, Tex.: Raintree Steck-Vaughn, 1999.

Pfeffer, Wendy. *Sounds All Around.* New York: HarperCollins, 1999.

Wright, Lynne. *The Science of Noise.* Austin, Tex.: Raintree Steck-Vaughn, 2000.

On the Web

For more information on *sound,* use FactHound to track down Web sites related to this book.

1. Go to *www.facthound.com*
2. Type in this book ID: 0756500923
3. Click on the *Fetch It* button.

Your trusty FactHound will fetch the best Web sites for you!

Through the Mail

The National Institute on Deafness and Other Communication Disorders (NIDCD)
National Institute of Health
31 Center Drive, MSC 2320
Bethesda, MD 20892-2320
To get information about how your ears work

On the Road

Discovery Museums
177 Main Street
Acton, MA 01720
978/264-4200
To visit an interesting sound exhibit

Index

About the Author

Darlene R. Stille is a science editor and writer. She has lived in Chicago, Illinois, all her life. When she was in high school, she fell in love with science. While attending the University of Illinois, she discovered that she also enjoyed writing. Today she feels fortunate to have a career that allows her to pursue both her interests. Darlene R. Stille has written more than thirty books for young people.